Contents

Executive Summary

Foster carers play a central role in providing family based care for foster children. Enabling, developing, and supporting foster carers to care for foster children in a way that provides security, stability, love and a strong sense of identity and belonging involves foster carers themselves being professionally supported, both emotionally and practically. This literature review focuses on 'social work support', and more particularly the role of the supervising social worker in providing that support and supervision. The discrete role of what we are refer to for the purposes of this literature review as the 'supervising social worker' (known by many others terms across the world), to provide supervision and support to foster carers, is a relatively recent development. Alongside the professionalisation of foster care, there have been changing views of the relationships and duties of supervising social workers and the introduction of criteria for supervision and inspection of fostering services. The expectations of the supervising social work role are set out in Standard 21 of the Fostering Services: National Minimum Standards in England (Department for Education, 2011). The supervising social worker acts as the conduit between the fostering household and the fostering service, and is distinct from the role of the foster child's social worker.

The role of the supervisory social worker is complex since it encompasses both the support and supervisory aspects of work done with the foster carer. For example, if a child protection matter is raised by a foster child's social worker, then the supervisory nature of the relationship between the foster carer and their supervising social worker becomes more prominent whereas when a foster carer experiences a family bereavement, the support relationship may take over. Foster carers report consistently that this relationship is very important to them and it has been shown to be a factor in the recruitment (in terms of the beliefs of potential carers about what support will be available) and retention of carers (Sebba, 2012). It is therefore of interest that the supervising social worker role has attracted little research or scholarly attention, perhaps because of the lack of well-developed models of supervising social work.

This review of the international research addresses the topic of the role of the supervising social worker. Foster care is considered in its broadest terms, including family and friends (kinship) foster care. The review was undertaken in order to consider the following three questions:

- What do supervising social workers do, and what are the components of supervision and support they offer foster carers?

- What contributes to effective supervision by social workers of foster carers?

- Does the quality and/or quantity of support and supervision offered to foster carers by supervising social workers impact on: outcomes for foster children; stability of placements; retention of foster carers?

Electronic databases and websites were used to identify 22 studies (24 related papers) from the UK, US, Canada and Australia. Comparisons across countries are subject to limitations of different cultures and services. Studies identified for the review were published since 1996 and were all in English. Fourteen of the 22 studies focused exclusively on foster carers' perceptions, the others focusing on social workers, caseworkers, foster family resource workers, fostering service managers and in one study young people, usually in addition to foster carers.

The studies used a range of methodologies from in-depth interviews and focus groups to larger scale surveys using questionnaires. Study samples ranged from 7 to nearly 2000 with only five studies reporting on data from samples of fewer than 30 participants. No studies were identified in the review that included interventions subjected to evaluation using comparison or control groups. Most studies adopted a retrospective design.

Key Findings

The support elements of the supervisory social worker's role have received much more attention in the literature to date than the supervisory nature of their relationship with foster carers. The evidence base includes studies that mainly research this relationship from the foster carers' perspective with relatively little attention given to the perceptions of the supervisory social workers or the fostering providers. Furthermore, there is very little focus on the impact that the relationship between supervisory social worker and foster carer has on placement stability or the outcomes for the child. Ultimately, child welfare and protection must take precedence.

Overall foster carers value the support that is provided to them by their fostering service and their supervising social worker. Emotional support was rated highly, alongside more practical elements. Carers appreciated social workers who were reliable and available, particularly at times of crisis, or stress; for example, around allegations and foster placement disruptions. Levels of contact were experienced, in the main, as indicating interest on behalf of the fostering services. Home visits were valued, as well as telephone contact. Foster carers appreciated support in relation to problematic contact for a foster child with their birth family. Respite arranged by the supervising social worker was seen by some foster carers as supportive. A number of foster carers believed that the workloads of supervising social workers affected their availability but no study reported data on workloads. While studies were limited in reporting the perspectives of the supervising social workers, there is no doubt (e.g. Sellick, 2013) that the increases in recording, regulation and compliance have changed the balance in their workload.

Foster carers and supervising social workers are members of the 'team around the child' supporting placing authorities with the planning and decision making for foster children, and the realisation of foster children's care plans. Foster carers voiced their wish to be included in decisions and planning relating to their foster children; and that their attachment to a foster child, and their foster child's attachment to them, should be taken into consideration in planning a child's future. A tension emerged regarding how foster carers were viewed within the professional network; whether or not they were seen, and worked with, as colleagues. Foster carers wanted to be trusted, respected and valued by supervising social workers. Joint training was seen by some as a way of including foster carers in the team. Foster carers valued effective interpersonal communication with their supervising social workers though it should be acknowledged that there remains a power imbalance since supervising social workers maintain an accountability for the carer's actions, which they review regularly. Foster carers also wanted as much information as possible about prospective children who were being considered for placement with them, and their current foster child. Foster carers also valued supervising social workers knowing their foster child, and their input in helping a foster carer manage troubled behaviour.

Other conclusions that can be drawn from this review are:

- Foster carers in general had a more positive view of their working relationships with their supervising social worker than they did with their foster child's social worker. When carers felt that supervising social workers and children's social workers worked well together this was perceived as helpful;

- Social work education and training were thought to need a more explicit focus on foster care, to adequately prepare both children's social workers and supervising social workers to work in foster care covering family placements and systemic practice;

- Placement disruptions were considered to have various contributory factors. Support to foster placements, in one study, was linked to placement stability (Tregeagle, Cox, Forbes, Humphreys and O'Neill, 2011), but in another not (Taylor and McQuillan, 2014);

- Some differences were noted between independent fostering services and public fostering services. Foster carers in the independent foster care sector felt particularly well supported;

- Supervision of supervising social workers was reported to need to include discussion about the personal attitudes of the social workers, to make sure that their attitudes did not affect decision-making;

- Retention of foster carers in many of the studies was reported to be linked to the quality and quantity of the support received by the foster carer in general, and in particular that provided by the supervising social worker.

Recommendations for policy and practice

Recommendations for further research

Given the limited research evidence regarding the role of the supervising social worker, recommendations can only be tentative.

- Foster carers value their relationships with their supervising social workers. Fostering services should therefore provide caseload management that ensures the availability of supervising social workers to work directly with foster carers, and provide supervision of those social workers that enhances their effectiveness;

- Practice guidance beyond the Minimum Standards in England needs to include the expectations of the supervising social worker role including the sometimes conflicting aspects of their relationship with the foster carer;

- The potential role of supervising social workers in the planned personal and professional development of foster carers needs to be further recognised;

- Public and independent fostering services need to consider ways of enhancing the working relationships between supervising social workers, foster children's social workers and foster carers, by the use of such concrete activities as joint training;

- Social work education and training needs to include knowledge and skills development pertinent to foster care.

The review identified a number of gaps and weaknesses in the existing research evidence noted above. We recommend that further research is undertaken that:

- Identifies and maps what the supervising social worker role encompasses; what supervising social workers do, day by day including caseload management, what is mandated and what is left to chance, within their fostering service, with other agencies and professionals and in their direct work with foster carers, foster children and the foster carers' family;

- Includes the perspectives of the supervising social workers;

- Considers the effectiveness of supervising social workers' interventions with foster carers and foster children, with particular respect to placement stability and the quality of the foster care experience;

- Draws on prospective research designs with comparison groups, to examine whether or not a fostering service, and supervising social worker, when informed by particular models of intervention and theoretical frameworks, makes a beneficial difference to outcomes for foster carers and foster children;

- Examines the quality of working relationships between supervising social workers and foster children's social workers, to see which aspects of their relationships make a difference to the experiences of foster carers and foster children, particularly regarding the management of allegations, disruptions, and the stability of placements;

- Addresses the experiences, and perceptions, of ethnic minority and indigenous foster carers, and those with health concerns, as well as their supervising social workers, regarding the usefulness of supervising social workers' support and supervision.

Main Report

Background to review

Foster care matters. It matters because a significant proportion of children in public care are placed with foster carers, therefore ensuring the number, quality, and stability of those children's foster care placements is a key responsibility of those accountable for foster children. The stability and permanence of placements for children has been of concern for decades; revisited in the United Kingdom (UK) context in 2013: *'The work of the Inquiry left us in no doubt that the 'care system' continues to fail too many children and families, and that tackling this problem is increasingly urgent and requires a fresh approach'* (Care Inquiry, 2013, p.2). The same Inquiry report went on to note that children need *'security, stability, love and a strong sense of identity and belonging'* (2013, p.7) when they are cared for by the State. Foster carers play a central role in providing family based care for foster children who, in the main, have troubled histories, sometimes leading to distressed and difficult behaviours. Enabling, developing, and supporting foster carers to care for foster children in such a way that provides 'security, stability, love and a strong sense of identity and belonging' involves foster carers themselves being professionally supported, both emotionally and practically. Sinclair (2005) identified eight core components for fostering services' provision of support to foster carers as follows: finance; training and preparation; carer groups; social work support; night duty teams; short breaks; preparation for placements; and teamwork. This literature review's focus is on 'social work support', and more particularly the role of the supervising social worker in providing that support, and supervision.

The discrete role of what we are referring to for the purposes of this literature review as the 'supervising social worker' (known by many others terms across the world, for example 'foster family resource worker in Canada; Brown, Rodgers and Anderson, 2014), to provide supervision and support to foster carers, is a relatively recent development. In England, the expectations of the supervising social work role is set out in Standard 21 of the Fostering Services: National Minimum Standards in England (DfE, 2011). The supervising social worker provides both supervision and support, and acts as the conduit between the fostering household and the fostering service, and is separate from the role of the foster child's social worker. By the 1990s this separation of the roles of the social worker working with the foster carer, and the social worker working with the foster child, seems to have become common practice (Sellick, 1999) in many countries. It is therefore of interest that the supervising social worker role has attracted little research or scholarly attention.

Over the last three decades the supervising social worker has been peripherally considered in research, chiefly through foster carers' perceptions of the role, embedded in research findings where the research focus was on another aspect of foster care (Aldgate and Bradley, 1999; Biehal, Ellison, Baker and Sinclair, 2010; Farmer, Moyers and Lipscombe, 2004; McSherry, Malet and Weatherall, 2013; Rowe, Cain, Hundleby and Keane, 1984; Schofield and Ward with Warman, Simmonds and Butler, 2008; Sinclair, Wilson and Gibbs, 2005; Wade, Sirriyeh, Kohli and Simmonds, 2012). Some publications aimed at social work practitioners (Collis, 1999; Lawson, 2011) and scholarly, discursive publications (Brown et al, 2014; Caw with Sebba, 2014; Fulcher and McGladdery, 2011; Sellick, 1999; Triseliotis, Sellick and Short, 1995) more directly addressed the supervisory, as well as the support, elements of the supervising social worker role. Lawson identified what he considered the necessary elements of the supervising social worker's supervision of foster carers as:

"providing information, advice and guidance; reviewing practical and emotional support needs; checking standards of care; responding to comments, concerns and allegations; ensuring compliance with policies and procedures; noting significant events and changes to the household; managing risk, health and safety and ensuring safer care; reviewing implementation of care plans for each child in placement; monitoring impact of fostering on the household; responding to carers' feedback and concerns; identifying and supporting learning and development needs; reviewing current and future use of resources; checking payments and equipment; reviewing records and reviewing carer's relationship with children placed".

(2011, p.37)

The complexity of the role has been commented upon, holding as it does both the support and supervisory aspects of work done with the foster carer, which at different times might be variously foregrounded (Brown et al, 2014; Fulcher and McGladdery, 2011; Wires, 1954). For example, if a standard of care, or child protection matter is raised by a foster child's social worker then the supervisory nature of the relationship between the foster carer and their supervising social worker becomes more prominent. In the UK context, the Government guidance about the supervising social worker (SSW) role emphasises the supervisory nature of this relationship: *'It is the SSW's role to supervise the foster carer's work, to ensure that they are meeting the child's needs, and to offer support and a framework to assess the foster carer's performance and develop their skills'* (H. M. Government, 2011, p.51). This focus on the supervisory nature of the supervising social worker/foster carer relationship seems to be less prominent in the research literature, where the support elements are more pronounced.

The economic and organisational context in which foster care takes place is likely to impact on the provision of, and perceptions about, the support and supervision provided to foster carers by fostering services. The high rate of social work staff turnover has been noted as a factor that can affect foster carers' experience of how they are supported by their fostering service and supervising social worker (Chipungu and Bent-Goodley, 2004; Claiborne, Auerbach, Lawrence, Liu, McGowna, Fernendes and Magnano, 2011). Foster carer perceptions regarding the quality of the support they get is one variable that appears to have a bearing on their retention (Wilson, Sinclair, Taylor, Pithouse and Sellick, 2004). In addition, given that 'the influence of existing foster carers on those considering fostering is also important' (Sebba, 2012, p.9), foster carers' views regarding the quality of the support and supervision they receive from their fostering service is relevant to the recruitment, as well as the retention, of foster carers (Cox, Buehler and Orme, 2002).

Research reviews encompassing foster carers' perceptions about social work support indicate that overall foster carers value the support they receive from their supervising social workers (Berridge, 1997; Sellick, Thoburn and Philpot, 2004; Wilson et al, 2004; Sinclair, 2005). This is important in relation to recruitment and retention of foster carers, both necessary concerns of fostering services. Social work support is particularly valued regarding matters that foster carers can experience as stressful; for example, contact with a foster child's birth family (Austerberry, Stanley, Larkins, Ridley, Farrelly, Manthorpe and Hussein, 2013). However, when we consider other areas of foster carer satisfaction, for example, that relating to training, in some cases where high levels of satisfaction have also been noted, this has not necessarily translated into improved outcomes for foster children (Pithouse, Young and Butler, 2002; Wilson et al, 2004). Two research studies indicated that carers reported that foster carer training can have a beneficial effect on both the quality of their parenting strategies and child outcomes, when associated with a coherent theoretical orientation, and delivered by a dedicated team, over a period of weeks; for example, the UK Fostering Changes 12 week training programme (Briskman, Castle, Blackeby, Bengo, Slack, Stebbens, Leaver and Scott, 2012), and the USA KEEP 16 week programme (Price, Chamberlain, Landsverk and Reid, 2009). These foster carer training and development programmes draw on particular theoretical approaches, a prerequisite that has also been noted as a necessary component of helpful supervision within social work and social care more generally (Hawkins and Shohet, 2012; Wonnacott, 2012). However, if foster carers' practice emanates from a coherent theoretical position we assume it is more likely to improve practice but further research is needed to test this out.

Appraising the support foster carers received, delivered by multidimensional treatment foster care teams, working to a specific theoretical approach and prescribed model, was one component of what was considered in a English evaluation of a number of multidimensional treatment foster care for adolescents programmes (Biehal et al, 2012; Green et al, 2014). However, in this study it was difficult to tease out the specific role of the supervising social worker from the overall support afforded the foster carers. Training and development of foster carers is different from their support and supervision; however, drawing on the early findings to date about the effectiveness of Fostering Changes and KEEP, we can surmise that a coherent model of supervision, underpinned by proven knowledge about effective team working, child development and childcare, might have a more beneficial impact on the direct care of foster children than otherwise. Texts describing a team approach to foster care, where the foster carer and supervising social worker are part of a professional team working to agreed goals, informed by a coherent theoretical approach, argue that this model of foster care is helpful for both foster carers and children (Caw with Sebba, 2014; Fulcher and McGladdery, 2011). However, robust research evidence to support this assertion remains sparse; which of course does not mean that it is not the case.

If the quality and quantity of support and supervision afforded foster carers by their supervising social workers are variables relevant to foster carer satisfaction, recruitment and retention, does the same hold for the impact this foster carer support and supervision has on outcomes for foster children and the stability of their placements? Research reviews to date indicate that there is limited evidence in this regard (Sinclair, 2005).

Aims and scope

This review of the international research addresses the topic of the role of the foster carer supervising social worker. The review considers foster care in its broadest terms, including family and friends (kinship) foster care. It was undertaken in order to consider the following three questions:

- What do supervising social workers do, and what are the components of supervision and support they offer foster carers?

- What contributes to effective supervision by social workers of foster carers?

- Does the quality and/or quantity of support and supervision offered to foster carers, by supervising social workers impact on: outcomes for foster children; stability of placements; retention of foster carers?

Methodology

This review synthesises the findings from the international literature on the role of the supervising social worker in foster care. A number of electronic databases were searched, including ASSIA, Australian Education Index, British Education Index, Campbell and Cochrane Libraries, Conference Proceedings Citation Index, ERIC, International Bibliography of Social Sciences, Medline, PsycInfo, SCOPUS, Social Care Online, Social Policy and Practice, Social Services Abstracts, and Social Sciences Citation Index.

The following websites were searched: BAAF, C4EO, Campbell, Casey Family Programs, Chapin Hall, Department for Education, EPPI, Joanna Briggs Institute, NCB, NFER, NSPCC, Office of Planning, Research and Evaluation in Administration for Children and Families (USA), SCIE, The Fostering Network, and What Works Clearinghouse.

Our search terms included:

"Supervising social worker*" OR "support social worker*" OR "link social worker*" OR "link worker*" OR "support worker*" OR "case worker*" OR "caseworker*"

and

"foster care" OR "foster carer*" OR "foster parent*" OR "foster famil*" OR "substitute famil*" OR "family foster home*" OR "out-of-home care" OR "looked after" OR "looked-after" OR "alternative care".

Titles and abstracts of the publications identified from the electronic searching were then screened for relevance. Finally, a range of international experts on foster care were contacted to suggest any references that were not uncovered by the electronic search. The review was restricted to empirical studies, though discursive papers informed the background, context and discussion. We did not restrict the review on the basis of particular kinds of methodology.

Status of the studies

The 24 research publications (22 related studies) in this review were selected from publications identified from 1954, but those eventually selected were published since 1996 and written in English. The studies were undertaken in the following countries; different contextual systems should be acknowledged which may limit transferability of some of the findings:

UK	9
USA	7
Canada	4
Australia	2

The studies included both qualitative and quantitative methods. Details of the studies can be found in Table 1 Appendix A.

Key Findings

The findings of this review start with the organisational context within which the supervising social work role is located before moving on to foster carers' perceptions of that role, and the support they receive. We then progress through a series of themes that emerged from undertaking the review.

As noted above, there is a body of work related to foster carer perceptions about what they find helpful in respect of social work support embedded in research reports, where the research focus was not directly about the role of the supervising social worker, but rather about another foster care question.

In the 24 papers (22 studies) we reviewed for this publication most of the findings in respect of our research questions are grouped under 'foster carer perceptions'. 'Support' and 'supervision' were rarely differentiated, and in some papers the term 'social work support' conflated the role of the child's social worker and that of the supervising social worker, reflecting the combined role that is practised in some other countries, so it proved hard to distinguish which role was being considered. Many of the themes overlapped, and the differentiations we have constructed are to some extent artificial, but enable the necessary emphasis on particular findings and, where relevant, the detail of some material within the reviewed publications to be visible.

Organisational context

Support and supervision takes place within particular national and organisational contexts. One of the features of this review was the overall similarity regarding emerging themes across nations. The findings do, however, illuminate some perceived differences between public foster care provision and that provided by the private, charitable and independent sectors which, for the purposes of this review, we refer to as independent fostering services.

Under the theme of organisational context we have included the differences that emerged regarding public and independent fostering provision; supervision of supervising social workers; workloads of supervising social workers and their frequency of visits to foster carers.

What supervising social workers do?

Two studies that explicitly asked what supervising social workers (foster parent resource workers in Canada) actually do were those undertaken by Brown et al (2014) and Gleeson and Philbin (1996). The Gleeson and Philbin study is about kinship foster carers, and in the write up of the research the 'caseworker' role was, as far as could be ascertained, conflating the roles of children's social worker and supervising social worker. What these 'caseworkers' did included: accessing resources for families, foster carers and children; assessing the needs of families, foster carers and children; and determining the permanence plan. Good case management and building relationships with the families were identified as important.

Brown et al (2014, no page no.) in Canada was the only study identified that asked the 'social workers' themselves, in this case 'foster parent resource workers', what they did. They identified 10 aspects of the role: 'monitor placement, facilitate communication between parties, teach communication skills, match foster homes and foster children, retain foster parents, promote teamwork, address problems with placements, support foster families, exercise authority, and ensure smooth operation'. While their role was distinct from the child's social worker they were involved in matching children to carers by drawing on their knowledge of the carers' qualities.

Tregeagle et al (2011) examined the time supervising social workers spent supporting foster placements, but the paper did not identify specifically what the social workers did, other than to differentiate 'contact' with foster carers from 'administration'. The 'direct contact' work with foster carers was not examined with regard to its component parts.

The frequency of supervising social worker visits in the Wade et al (2012) study was on average monthly, and in Clarke (2009) was between four to six weeks. Fisher et al (2000) found a relationship between the frequency of visits and foster carers feeling supported by their supervising social workers. The pacing of social work visits was considered by Maclay, Bunce and Purves (2006) and Tregeagle et al (2011). Maclay et al noted that the foster carers in the study said that they became more assertive over time with social workers, and were therefore able to challenge them, and seek support when needed. Tregeagle et al (2011) described a model of social work support designed to give more direct social work contact to foster carers in the first year of a placement, and for more challenging placements. They also commented on the need for flexibility in providing higher levels of direct contact with fostering households when needed.

Supervision of supervising social workers

Wonnacott (2012), and Hawkins and Shohet (2012), emphasise the importance of social workers being supervised within the context of a theoretical framework, enabling them to work effectively with service users and carers. Useful supervision of supervising social workers might too need to be located within a theoretical framework, involving reflective practice within enabling organisations, committed to the development of their social workers, and their foster carers, to be effective (Caw with Sebba, 2014).

In this review the studies that included the subject of supervision of social workers in most depth were Gleeson and Philbin (1996), and Hollingsworth, Bybee, Johnson and Swick (2010). The supervisors of the social workers thought that most were ill prepared, through their education and training, to work with the complexity of family and friends foster care. They viewed their limitations as relating to their knowledge of the legal and policy framework, and theoretical approaches that would enhance their interventions. The supervisors also recorded that, in their view, they spent an 'enormous amount of time' (1996, p.30) preparing social workers to work with family and friends foster carers. Another aspect of supervision remarked upon by supervisors was that they had to focus on the writing skills of the social workers. The Gleeson and Philbin paper emphasised the educational role of the supervisor, particularly in relation to clinical intervention skills development via discussion about individual foster carers and their foster children.

Hollingsworth et al (2010) conclude with points they considered important for supervisors to hold in mind when supervising social workers working in foster care, including: that the opinions of the social worker might influence their decision making; and the need to make sure that decision making in foster care was informed by knowledge underpinned by research.

Workloads

The pressure of work, and size of workloads for supervising social workers was a matter for comment in a number of the studies (Rosenwald and Bronstein, 2008; Chuang, Wells, Green and Reiter, 2011; Maclay et al, 2006). In the Maclay et al and Rosenwald and Bronstein studies, the foster carers viewed the size of their supervising social workers' caseloads as a reason why they might not be as available to them as they otherwise could be.

Differences between independent fostering services and public fostering services

This review revealed a number of perceived differences between public and independent foster care provision about the role of the supervising social worker.

As noted above Tregeagle at al's (2011) study was located within an Australian NGO using a model of social work support intervention; this meant that the frequency of visits to foster carers was planned according to the length of the placement, as well as its complexity. This pattern of planned visits to a fostering household was perceived to lessen the likelihood of placement disruption.

Independent fostering service foster carers overall felt more valued than their public foster carer colleagues in the Kirton, Beecham and Ogilvie (2007) study. Wade et al (2012) found that most of their foster carers from the independent fostering services generally felt well supported. These findings have to be set in the context of other studies in which it was found that overall the majority of foster carers felt supported, irrespective of whether their fostering service was independent or public (Clarke, 2009); other than in the Okeke (2003) study.

Kirton et al's findings uncovered differences between how foster carers from the independent and public sectors viewed how they felt they were listened to and supported:

"IFP responses were markedly more positive than those from LAs. Seventy per cent of the study's 170 IFP carers stated that they felt valued as colleagues and 61 per cent that they felt their agencies listened and responded to carers' concerns".

(2007, p.8)

It is also noteworthy that in this study the foster carers feeling 'valued and listened to', did not necessarily equate with placement stability. Another interesting finding from the same study was the independent fostering service supervising social workers seemingly being more open to working with foster carers as 'colleagues', than were their public fostering service colleagues.

Hollingsworth et al (2010) compared the characteristics, attitudes and beliefs of social workers in public and independent fostering services. Pertinent to this review they found that social workers in the independent sector held more negative attitudes towards birth parents who suffered from mental ill health, and drug and alcohol misuse. How transferable those findings are to foster care is not known. Hollingsworth et al recommend that these findings are taken into account in supervision of those working in foster care, as they might affect attitudes of supervising social workers towards contact with birth families.

Foster carer perception

Of the 24 publications (22 studies) selected for review, 19 had as a central feature the 'perception of foster carers' regarding the support they were given by their fostering service, their foster child's social worker and their supervising social worker. As noted above support was emphasised, rather than supervision, though what they meant by 'support' might have differed significantly from carer to carer. The research findings were drawn from very different research designs, and sample sizes, as can be seen from Table 1, Appendix A. Different studies therefore carry more or less weight regarding the transferability of their findings. Nonetheless, irrespective of geographical location, when the research was undertaken, the research design, or sample size, some of the findings were strikingly similar. Foster carers felt that if they were 'supported', that support benefitted them, but also the children and young people in their care: *'where professional support was reliable, predictable and responsive, foster carers felt that they and the young people in their care benefitted considerably'* (Wade et al, 2012, p.277).

Emotional support

Being a foster carer is a difficult role, and the dominant theme arising from the research findings was the importance of the emotional support that foster carers received, enabling them to fulfil that role. From the 19 publications which drew on foster carer perceptions of the support they received, emotional support was noted as a key facet that foster carers valued. The relationship with their supervising social worker appeared to have been a key vehicle by which they experienced emotional support, amongst others for example, support from their own families (Sinclair, Gibbs and Wilson, 2004). Hudson and Levasseur (2002) noted that slightly more foster carers valued emotional support over practical support. Conversely, for other foster carers, although they valued emotional support they also wanted action as well as listening (Triseliotis, Borland and Hill, 2000). Lack of emotional support, was one factor associated with foster carers resigning (Macgregor, Rodger, Cummings and Leschied, 2006). Interestingly in the Hudson and Levasseur (2002) study the fostering service thought they were not meeting the foster carers' emotional support needs as well as they might.

Practical support

Practical support, although different from emotional support, was often cited alongside emotional support as being one aspect of the two components foster carers viewed as comprising effective support. The importance of practical support for foster carer satisfaction was present in a number of papers (Fisher, Gibbs, Sinclair and Wilson, 2000; Hudson and Levasseur, 2002; Macgregor et al, 2006).

Availability and reliability

Given the nature of foster carers' role, involving as it does caring for foster children who have often experienced separation and trauma, within the private space of the foster carer's domestic sphere and family, it is of little surprise that foster carers rate highly the availability and reliability of social work support. This aspect of support featured in many of the publications reviewed (Brown, Moraes and Mayhew, 2005; Cavazzi, Guilfoyle and Sims, 2010; Clarke, 2009; Fisher et al, 2000; Hudson and Levasseur, 2002; Macgregor et al, 2006; Taylor and McQuillan, 2014; Sinclair et al, 2004; Triseliotis et al, 2000). Direct contact with social workers was valued, but telephone contact was also appreciated, because it conveyed interest (Brown et al, 2005; Fisher et al, 2000; Sinclair et al, 2004). However, in one study too much telephone contact was experienced by some foster carers as problematic (Fisher et al, 2000). Foster carers particularly valued available and reliable support if they had an allegation made against them, and lack of support contributed to feelings of dissatisfaction (Fisher et al, 2000; Kirton et al, 2007; Triseliotis et al, 2000).

Home visits

Although telephone contact was appreciated by many foster carers, home visits were still seen as important by foster carers (Brown, 2008; Brown et al, 2005; Hudson and Levasseur, 2002; Kirton et al, 2007; Macgregor et al, 2006; Sinclair et al, 2004; Triseliotis et al, 2000; Wade et al, 2012). The duration, as well as the frequency of visits, was noted in one study as being significant for foster carers (Kirton et al, 2007).

Contact

Foster children's birth family contact has been identified as a potential area of stress for foster carers (Austerberry et al, 2013), and one where they appreciate support; this was borne out in the publications reviewed (Fisher et al, 2000; Taylor and McQuillan, 2014; Triseliotis et al, 2000). In the Taylor and McQuillan (2014) study, which addressed disruptions in foster placements, over half the foster carers thought that contact had contributed to disruptions; therefore supervision and support to foster carers related to contact might be significant.

Crisis

Foster carers being able to access support during a crisis was a theme that emerged in the studies (Cavazzi et al, 2010; Hudson and Levasseur, 2002; Macgregor et al, 2006; Triseliotis et al, 2000). This often linked with their perceptions of the availability of their social worker. In one study psychologists were seen as giving a better crisis response than social workers (Cavazzi et al, 2010).

Respite

Respite for foster carers (short-term fostering by another carer to provide the main carer with a break) is not provided by supervising social workers, but it is usually arranged by them and their fostering service. Many foster carers in the studies perceived respite as being an element of support that they appreciated; which made a difference to their perception of the support offered by the fostering service. In some cases foster carers said that they would have liked more respite (Hudson and Levasseur, 2002; Macgregor et al, 2006; Triseliotis et al, 2000).

Summary

Foster carers' perceptions about what they want from their fostering service, and supervising social workers, are important to note because their views, as we note later, can impact on retention. As the key players in foster care it is valuable to garner their opinions. Their perceptions inform fostering services and social workers about areas of strengths in their social work provision, and where they could develop further. Two papers drawn from the same study provide useful summaries regarding foster carer perceptions of social work support as follows:

"This paper has described the qualities which foster carers seek from social workers. In general, the foster carers in our sample had views consistent with those identified in the literature. In their eyes good social workers: show an interest in how carers are managing; are easy to contact and responsive when contacted; do what they say they are going to do; are prepared to listen and offer encouragement; take account of the family's needs and circumstances; keep them informed and included in planning; ensure that payments, complaints, etc. are processed as soon as possible; attend to the child's interests and needs, and involve foster carers in this where appropriate."

(Fisher et al, 2000, p.231)

Sinclair et al note:

"The carers' requirements of these social workers were simple and understandable. They should respect the carer, visit promptly when asked, be efficient and expeditious in sorting out difficulties with the local authority, listen to both child and carer, work as a team with the carer, do what they promise and provide good advice".

(2004, p. 115)

Team around the foster child

Foster carers want to be part of the 'team' (Sinclair et al, 2004); to be part of the group of professionals responsible for the care, decision making, and planning for a foster child; 'the team around the child'. This seems particularly pertinent because foster carers live with and care for their foster child on a day-to-day basis, and in most cases know the child better than any of the other professionals involved. Although the theme of 'team around the child' does not immediately appear directly related to the role of the supervising social worker, it does impact on how the supervising social worker conceptualises, as well as actualises, their work with foster carers. Caw with Sebba (2014) describe a Team Parenting model in which carers are the agents of change for the child. If the members of the team around the child are committed to this role of the carer, it can change the way social workers behave. There were a number of key areas we identified that we have grouped under this theme as follows:

Planning and decision-making

A number of studies identified the importance foster carers placed on being part of planning and decision-making for the foster children they cared for (Brown, 2008; Brown et al, 2014; Fisher et al, 2000; Gleeson and Philbin, 1996; Hudson and Levasseur, 2002; Kirton et al, 2007; Macgregor et al, 2006; Rhodes, Orme and Buehler, 2001; Wilson, Sinclair and Gibbs, 2000). Indeed involvement with the team, and being part of decision making and planning was seen, in some cases, as related to foster carers' willingness to managing more challenging placements. *'Foster parents are more likely to be willing to handle more frustration in dealing with difficult children if they feel integrated as part of the child welfare team'* (Macgregor et al, 2006, p.364). Where there were differences of view, or conflicts, between the foster carer and those making decisions, or plans, for foster children this was experienced as a particular difficulty by foster carers. One role of the supervising social worker is to advocate on behalf of the foster carer at the child's review. The importance of the attachment between foster carers and their foster children was highlighted; foster carers thought its significance was given too little attention in decision-making and planning (Cavazzi et al, 2010).

Timing and arrangement of meetings

A number of studies commented on foster carers' frustration when they were not consulted regarding the timing and location of meetings. When the arrangements had already been made, and the foster carer was expected to fit in, this conveyed the message that they were not considered key players or equal professionals in the team responsible for the care of a foster child (Kirton et al, 2007).

Foster carer as 'client' or 'colleague'

A debate that was evident in some of the research papers, relevant to how foster carers and supervising social workers perceive one another, as well as work with each other, was the question of whether or not foster carers are considered by children's social workers, and supervising social workers, as being professional colleagues. With the increasing professionalisation of foster care this was a potential tension in working relationships, when foster carers felt themselves to be fellow professionals in the team around the child, but were not viewed in the same light by social workers (Hudson and Levasseur, 2002; Kirton et al, 2007; Sheldon, 2004). This ambiguous relationship seemed to be fundamental to the difficulties some foster carers experienced working with social workers as equal professional partners. Social workers in one study articulated their ambivalence as being related to the supervisory nature of the foster carer/social worker relationship: *'I'm really not sure about this one. Partners— yes, but the relationship cannot be a truly equal partnership'* (Sheldon, 2004, p.29). Another commented, *'this is all Okay until something goes wrong'* (Sheldon, 2004, p.31), perhaps reflecting the fact that child protection takes precedence over all other functions. Kirton et al (2007) contextualise this debate as related to how foster carers have been viewed differently over time, and how historically they were often viewed as 'clients', rather than colleagues. In Kirton et al's (2007) study the independent fostering service supervising social workers were more likely to view their foster carers as colleagues, than the social workers drawn from local authority fostering services.

Joint training

Joint training for foster carers and supervising social workers, as well as with children's social workers, can be important to signify partnership working (Kirton et al, 2007). Having foster carers delivering training was also perceived as being useful by some foster carers (Macgregor et al, 2006).

Trust

The theme of trust was evident in some studies (Hudson and Levasseur, 2002; Macgregor et al, 2006; and Rosenwald and Bronstein, 2008); foster carers feeling that they were not sufficiently trusted, and this lack of trust then affecting how they were engaged with as professional colleagues within the team responsible for the care plan for the foster child. Trust for foster carers was closely linked to feeling valued by supervising social workers and fostering services.

Being valued and respected

The importance for foster carers of feeling valued and respected by their supervising social workers, and fostering services, featured in a number of studies (Hudson and Levasseur, 2002; Kirton et al, 2007; Rosenwald and Bronstein, 2008; Taylor and McQuillan, 2014). Noteworthy are two findings in the Kirton et al (2007) study. First, they found that overall the independent fostering service foster carers felt more valued and respected than their local authority foster carer colleagues. Second, *'Feeling valued and listened to were also found to be associated with carers' health ratings…'* (Kirton et al, 2007, p.8). Both these findings are open to interpretations not offered in the papers. For example, the role of the supervising social worker may require the carer to respect being challenged at times so unconditional positive regard for the carer might not reflect the balance needed. However, this was not mentioned in the research reviewed and therefore would need further scrutiny prior to drawing conclusions.

Information about the foster child

The information made available to foster carers about foster children they might look after, or those that they already cared for, appeared from the studies to be an area of contention, and in the cases of foster carers thinking they were given too little information, an area that foster carers associate with not being trusted, valued partners in the team around the child (Cavazzi et al, 2010; Clarke, 2009; Fisher et al, 2000; Kirton et al, 2007; Macgregor et al, 2006; Rosenwald and Bronstein, 2008; Sheldon, 2004; Taylor and McQuillan, 2014; Triseliotis et al, 2000; Wilson et al, 2000). A key role then for the supervising social worker might be to 'broker' information about the child and to help the carer understand and interpret that information.

Communication

The quality of interpersonal communication between the foster carer and their supervising social worker is likely to be a critical aspect of the effectiveness of how they work together. Communication was a theme that emerged in a number of studies (Macgregor et al, 2006; Okeke, 2003; Rhodes et al, 2001; Sheldon, 2004; Taylor and McQuillan, 2014). When communication emerged, where foster carers felt valued, trusted and part of the team around the child, they were also likely to perceive the quality of their communication as good between themselves and their supervising social worker. Taylor and McQuillan, commenting on their findings regarding communication between foster carers, supervising social workers and children's social workers wrote: *'The data on communication were largely positive. It is unsurprising that the three participant groups had slightly higher opinions of their own communication than others!'* (2014, p.246). Okeke, in the conclusion of his study, notes the importance of helping relationship skills for supervising social workers when working with foster carers (he refers to 'foster mothers' as this group was the focus of his study): *'…communicating respect through commitment, empathy, warmth, avoiding the rush to critical judgement, and reinforcing foster mothers' strengths…'* (2003, p.276).

Supervising social worker's familiarity, and work with the foster child

In a number of the studies foster carers gaining sufficient guidance, and support, when helping children with troubling, and problematic behaviour was raised; some foster carers thinking that they did not get sufficient help. The delineated roles of the supervising social worker working with the foster carer, and child's social worker working with the foster child, means that in many cases the focus on the child's behaviour lies with the foster child's social worker. However, as noted earlier the English government guidance for the supervising social worker role requires supervising social workers to ensure that the foster carer is *'meeting the child's needs'*; it is difficult to envisage how the supervising social worker would do this without engaging with both the foster carer and the foster child, particularly when the child's behaviour is seen as problematic by the foster carer. Not surprisingly supporting foster carers with managing children's behaviour featured in many of the studies (Brown et al, 2005; Fisher et al, 2000; Hudson and Levasseur, 2002; Kirton et al, 2007; Sinclair et al, 2004; Rhodes et al, 2001; Taylor and McQuillan, 2014). In one study foster carers', supervising social workers' and foster children's social workers' different opinions were recorded about foster carers' management of foster children's problematic behaviour. Some of the foster children's social workers (in the study referred to as FSW) thought foster carers had limited understanding of children's behaviour:

"The primary theme from FSWs concerned their opinion that foster carers were limited in understanding, responding to and managing children's behaviour appropriately. Foster parents primarily named and described the behaviours and were predominantly negative about the children and their "problems". SSWs showed a mix of both FSW and foster carer themes. They also named the behaviours and acknowledged these as being complex. Some SSWs also thought that foster carers' behaviour management could have been improved".

(Taylor and McQuillan, 2014, p.240)

It is of course possible that there was a relationship between the lack of support and supervision some foster carers thought they got from their supervising social worker and the foster child's social worker about managing a foster child's behaviour, and social workers' perceptions of foster carers' limited understanding about and skills to beneficially affect a child's behaviour. However, to evidence a clear relationship between the two would need further research. In the field of foster carer training some initial findings have been positive about the relationship between inputs to foster carers, through foster carer training programmes regarding: understanding of children's behaviour; how those children's experiences might impact upon behaviour; how to help children change their behaviour, and foster carers' changed approaches to managing children's behaviour (Briskman et al, 2012; Price et al, 2009).

Relationships between foster carers, children's social workers and supervising social workers

Effective working relationships between all members of the team around the child are considered a necessary component of effective foster care and should include the supervising social worker empathising with, and sometimes challenging the foster carer. Studies that looked at foster carers' perceptions about the quality of working relationships between themselves, their supervising social worker, and the foster child's social worker found that most foster carers felt that they had a better working relationship with their supervising social worker than they did with their foster child's social worker (Clarke, 2009; Kirton et al, 2007; Ramsay, 1996; Sinclair et al, 2004; Wade et al, 2012). An important finding in the Wade et al study was that: *'Support from SSWs was pivotal and highly rated, although black and Asian foster carers appeared rather more ambivalent about this role than were white foster carers"* (Wade et al, 2012, p.277). Okeke (2003) found that overall his sample of 30 African-American foster carers also felt less positive about their relationships with their supervising social workers. This might be an aspect of the supervising social worker/foster carer relationship that needs further research exploration.

In Sheldon's study (2004) he found that there were some difficulties in the working relationships between children's social workers and supervising social workers, and these difficulties were concentrated into the areas of communication, clarity regarding roles, and expectations about what foster carers could reasonably manage. The effective working relationship between the foster child's social worker and the supervising social worker was noted by Wade et al (2012); foster carer satisfaction not surprisingly was increased when their fostered young person's social worker and their own supervising social worker worked well together. Overall for the supervising social worker, managing the relationships with both the foster carer and child's social worker and the dynamic between them, not to mention influencing the child's needs and how they are being met, illustrates the tensions in their role.

Social work education and training

The preparedness of social workers to work in foster care, through their social work education and training, was commented upon in three studies (Fisher et al, 2000; Hollingsworth et al, 2010; Sheldon, 2004). Fisher at al mention the need for social work education and training to emphasise the qualities and skills that foster carers appreciate. Furthermore, enabling and developing the supervisory social work skills involved in setting up a team, and group work, are not part of the usual social work training. Social worker readiness to practise in the fields of fostering and adoption has been a concern in the English context, and as a result a *'curriculum framework for continuing professional development (CPD) on planning and supporting permanence: reunification, family and friends care, long-term foster care, special guardianship and adoption'* was developed for the College of Social Work in 2013 (Schofield and Simmonds, 2013 p.1). It is too soon to evaluate if it will make a difference to how well people think social workers are educated and trained to work in foster care in the future. Chuang et al (2011) note that for social workers to be enabled to make use of training they receive, their organisational context needs to be interested in nurturing the knowledge and skills they have learnt and developed.

Placement disruptions

Permanence for children in public care and the stability of foster placements are subjects that have attracted research and policy attention for decades (Care Inquiry, 2013; Sinclair et al, 2005). Two of the studies in this review focussed explicitly on disruption of foster placements (Taylor and McQuillan, 2014; Tregeagle et al, 2011). Foster carers articulating a link between their decisions to stop fostering and disruption of a placement was recorded in the Wilson et al (2000) study. In the conclusion of their study Fisher et al (2000) comment on the need for social workers to proactively engage with potential disruptions, to manage the tendency for splitting when allegations are made, and when disruptions in placements occur: *'to treat disrupted placements seriously and with care, that is, to acknowledge and engage with the feelings of the child and of the carers'* (2000, p.232).

In the Taylor and McQuillan (2014) study which defines a disruption as an unplanned ending irrespective of whether it is an emergency, short or long-term, over half the foster carers thought that contact between their foster child and the child's birth family had contributed to disruption. Hence, supervision and support to foster carers around contact might be significant, as noted earlier. In the same study the importance of: *'Listening to and supporting foster carers and helping them to feel valued as opposed to "failures" following disruptions were prominent themes across all participant groups'* (2014, pp.241-242). This is an important message for supervising social workers, and their fostering services, who can feel frustrated with their foster carer following the unplanned ending of a placement. In the same study data from foster children's social workers, foster carers, and supervising social workers indicated that most thought that many foster placements disrupt, irrespective of the level of support provided. They also found in their sample that a slightly higher number of placements disrupted where the placement had been planned, than those made in an emergency (which flies in the face of received wisdom), and that placements were more likely to disrupt within the first year, and more specifically within the first four months.

Some of Taylor and McQuillan's findings differed, to some degree, from those of Tregeagle et al (2011). The Tregeagle et al study, looking at the costs of sustaining the stability of foster placements, concluded that support did make a difference to stability for unstable placements, and for placements in their first year. The intensive support input in the first year of a placement was seen, by the Non-Governmental Organisation (NGO) service where Tregeagle et al's research was undertaken, as being a necessary

preventative intervention to sustain stability, and for establishing relationships, to make sure that small issues did not build up. This organisation had a defined model of social work support intervention, framed within a theoretical framework of permanence. However, a causal relationship between support and supervision of foster carers, informed by a theoretical framework, improving stability in placements has yet to be proven.

Retention of foster carers

A number of studies in this review made the link between perceived notions of adequate and inadequate support that foster carers received from their fostering service, and their supervising social workers, as well as from their foster child's social worker, and retention (Fisher et al, 2000; Hudson and Levasseur, 2002; Macgregor et al, 2006; Maclay et al, 2006; Ramsay, 1996; Rhodes et al, 2001; Sinclair et al, 2004; Triseliotis et al, 2000; Wilson et al, 2000). Lack of support to foster carers, in its broadest sense, was the main reason given by foster carers for either giving up, or thinking of giving up, fostering (Maclay et al, 2006; Rhodes et al, 2001). In the Rhodes et al study approximately a third of foster carers who were no longer fostering, or who were considering stopping, cited a poor working relationship with their supervising social worker as being a contributory factor. This point was reiterated in the Fisher et al study: *'Our findings suggest that good relationships with family placement workers do influence decisions to continue fostering'* (2000, p.232). However, Sinclair et al (2004) caution against a causal relationship being drawn between poor support from the supervising social worker, and the fostering service, leading to poor retention of foster carers when they write:

"Social workers and link workers are therefore highly important elements in the foster carers' system of support. However, commitment to fostering, decisions to leave fostering and the carer's mental health are subject to a wide range of influences over and above the formal support the carer receives. In relation to these broader outcomes, social workers play a much smaller, although arguably significant part".

(2004, p.117)

Gaps in the current research evidence base

Whilst undertaking this review we identified a number of gaps in the existing research informing social work and foster care practice, as it relates to the role of the supervising social worker. We know quite a lot about what foster carers think about social work support, and what they find useful. But we still know surprisingly little about what supervising social workers think they do, what they actually do, and if what they do is effective in supporting foster carers and foster children. We know even less about whether or not their interventions increase the likelihood of placement stability, and improve the quality of foster care for foster children. We were unable therefore to adequately answer any of our questions that we hoped to address through this literature review; although it has thrown some light on aspects of the supervising social work role, and certainly how it is perceived by foster carers.

The foci of the studies in this review were primarily about the 'support' elements of the supervising social worker role, rather than the supervisory ones. This is likely to be the case because much of the research evidence drew on foster carers' and not supervising social workers', retrospective and not current, perceptions. This also means that the possible tension between the supervisory social worker providing support and challenging the foster carer when appropriate did not emerge.

Most of the research studies were retrospective, descriptive studies. To provide evidence of the usefulness of the supervising social worker role, we argue, there would need to be prospective research undertaken, exploring all aspects of the role of the supervising social worker, and how that role is performed. Such research studies might usefully consider whether or not a fostering service and supervising social worker being informed by a particular model of intervention, and theoretical framework, makes a difference to outcomes for foster carers and foster children. Sinclair et al (2005) argue that helping foster carers to manage children's behaviour in placements needs to be informed by appropriate theory. We surmise that this might also be the case for informing supervising social workers in their role of supporting, and supervising, foster carers and foster children. The efficacy of our assertion needs testing through research studies involving prospective designs, and the use of comparison groups and the perceptions of the supervising social workers themselves and their managers.

We identified a need to look in more depth at the working relationships between supervising social workers and the foster child's social worker, to examine in more depth if the quality of that working relationship makes a difference to the experiences of foster carers, particularly regarding the management of allegations, disruptions and the stability of placements.

We noted that two studies (Okeke, 2003; Wade et al, 2012) identified that ethnic minority and indigenous carers in their studies felt less effectively supported. This was also the case for foster carers with health concerns (Kirton et al, 2007), a similar finding arose in Austerberry et al's (2013) findings; these findings might be worth further exploration and scrutiny.

The review provided as much information about the gaps in the existing research evidence, regarding the role of the supervising social worker, as it did material. However, it revealed a detailed picture of how foster carers perceive 'support' from their social workers, and whether that support makes a difference to them.

Conclusions

Overall foster carers value the support that is provided to them by their fostering service and their supervising social worker. Emotional support was rated highly, alongside more practical elements. They appreciated social workers who were reliable, and available, particularly at times of crisis, or stress; for example, around allegations and foster placement disruptions. Levels of contact were experienced, in the main, as indicating interest on behalf of the fostering services. Home visits were valued, as well as telephone contact. Foster carers appreciated support in relation to problematic contact for a foster child with their birth family. Respite arranged by the supervising social worker was seen by some foster carers as supportive. A number of foster carers believed that the workloads of supervising social workers affected their availability although no study reported data on caseloads. While studies were limited in reporting the perspectives of the supervising social workers, there is no doubt (e.g. Sellick, 2013) that the increases in recording, regulation and compliance have changed the balance in their workload.

Foster carers and supervising social workers are members of the 'team around the child' supporting placing authorities with the planning and decision making for foster children, and the realisation of foster children's care plans. Foster carers voiced their wish to be included in decisions and planning relating to their foster children; and that their attachment to a foster child, and their foster child's attachment to them, should be taken into consideration in planning a child's future. A tension emerged regarding how foster carers were viewed within the professional network; whether or not they were seen, and worked with, as colleagues. Foster carers wanted to be trusted, respected and valued by supervising social workers as suggested in models that recognise them as the agents for change but for the supervising social worker the power imbalance in the relationship with the foster carer remains, given their supervisory duties. Joint training was seen by some as a way of including foster carers in the team. Foster carers valued effective interpersonal communication with their supervising social workers. They also wanted as much information as possible about prospective children who were being considered for placement with them, and their current foster child. Foster carers also valued supervising social workers knowing their foster child, and their input in helping a foster carer manage troubled behaviour.

Other conclusions that can be drawn from this review are:

- Foster carers in general had a more positive view of their working relationships with their supervising social worker than they did with their foster child's social worker. When carers felt that supervising social workers and children's social workers worked well together this was perceived as helpful;

- Social work education and training were thought to require an explicit focus on foster care, to adequately prepare both children's social workers, and supervising social workers, to work in foster care covering family placements and systemic practice;

- Placement disruptions were considered to have various contributory factors. Support to foster placements, in one study, was linked to placement stability (Tregeagle et al, 2011), but in another not (Taylor and McQuillan, 2014);

- Some differences were noted between independent fostering services and public fostering services. Foster carers felt well supported in the independent foster care sector;

- Supervision of supervising social workers was thought to need to include discussion about the personal attitudes of the social workers, to make sure that their attitudes did not affect decision-making;

- Retention of foster carers, in many of the studies was thought to be linked to the quality and quantity of the support that was afforded foster carers in general, and in particular that provided by the supervising social worker.

Recommendations for policy and practice

Recommendations for further research

Given the limited research evidence regarding the role of the supervising social worker, recommendations can only be tentative.

- Foster carers value their relationships with their supervising social workers. Fostering services should therefore provide caseload management that ensures the availability of supervising social workers to work directly with foster carers, and provide supervision of those social workers that enhances their effectiveness;

- Practice guidance beyond the Minimum Standards in England needs to include the expectations of the supervising social worker role including the sometimes conflicting aspects of their relationship with the foster carer;

- The potential role of supervising social workers in the planned personal professional development of foster carers needs to be further recognised;

- Public and independent fostering services to consider ways of enhancing the working relationships between supervising social workers, foster children's social workers and foster carers, by the use of such concrete events as joint training;

- Social work education and training to include knowledge and skills development pertinent to foster care.

The review identified a number of gaps and weaknesses in the existing research evidence noted above. We recommend that further research is undertaken that:

- Identifies, and maps, what the supervising social worker role encompasses; what supervising social workers do, day by day including caseload management, what is mandated and what is left to chance, within their fostering service, with other agencies and professionals, and in their direct work with foster carers, foster children and the foster carers' families;

- Includes the perspectives of the supervising social workers;

- Considers the effectiveness of supervising social workers' interventions with foster carers and foster children, with particular respect to placement stability and the quality of the foster care experience;

- Draws on prospective research designs with comparison groups, to examine whether or not a fostering service, and supervising social worker, when informed by a particular models of intervention and theoretical frameworks, makes a beneficial difference to outcomes for foster carers and foster children;

- Examines the quality of working relationships between supervising social workers, and foster children's social workers, to see which aspects of their relationships makes a difference to the experiences of foster carers and foster children, particularly regarding the management of allegations, disruptions, and the stability of placements;

- Addresses the experiences, and perceptions, of ethnic minority and indigenous foster carers, and those with health concerns, as well as their supervising social workers, regarding the usefulness of supervising social workers' support and supervision.

The Rees Centre is committed to providing robust, useful and timely research and will be consulting a wide range of stakeholders on the findings from this review and considering how to take these recommendations forward. We look forward to your comments.

Helen Cosis Brown
University of Bedfordshire

Judy Sebba
Director

Nikki Luke
Research Officer

Rees Centre for Research in Fostering and Education
rees.centre@education.ox.ac.uk

References

Aldgate, J. and Bradley, M. (1999). *Supporting families through short-term fostering,* London: The Stationery Office.

Austerberry, H., Stanley, N., Larkins, C., Ridley, J., Farrelly, N., Manthorpe, J. and Hussein, S. (2013). Foster carers and family contact: Foster carers' views of social work support, *Adoption and Fostering,* 37(2), pp.116-129.

Berridge, D. (1997). *Foster care: A research review,* London: The Stationary Office.

Biehal, N., Dixon, J., Parry, E. and Sinclair, I., Green, J., Roberts, C., Kay, C., Rothwell, J. Kapadia, D. and Roby, A. (2012). *The care placement evaluation (CaPE) evaluation of multidimensional treatment foster care for adolescents (MTFC-A),* London: Department of Education. Available at: https://www.gov.uk/government/uploads/system/uploads/attachment_data/file/249856/DFE-RR194.pdf (Accessed 8 July 2014).

Biehal, N., Ellison, S., Baker, C. and Sinclair, I. (2010). *Belonging and permanence: Outcomes in long-term foster care and adoption,* London: British Agencies for Adoption and Fostering.

Briskman, J., Castle, J., Blackeby, K., Bengo, C., Slack, K., Stebbens, C., Leaver, W. and Scott, S. (2012). *Randomised controlled trial of the Fostering Changes programme,* London: National Academy for Parenting Research, King's College London/Department of Education.

Brown, H. C. (2014). *Social work and foster care,* London: Sage/Learning Matters.

Brown, J. D. (2008). Foster parents' perceptions of factors needed for successful foster placements, *Journal of Children and Family Studies,* 17(4), pp.538-554.

Brown, J. D., Moraes, S. and Mayhew, J. (2005). Service needs of foster families with children who have disabilities, *Journal of Child and Family Studies,* 14(3), pp.417-429.

Brown, J. D., Rodgers, J. and Anderson, L. (2014). Roles of foster parent resource workers, *Journal of Child and Family Studies.* DOI 10.1007/s10826-014-9959-7 (Advance online publication).

Care Inquiry (2013). *Making not breaking: Building relationships for our most vulnerable children,* London: The Fostering Network.

Cavazzi, T., Guilfoyle, A. and Sims, M. (2010). A phenomenological study of foster caregivers' experiences of formal and informal support, *Illinois Child Welfare,* 5(1) pp.125-141.

Caw, J. with Sebba, J. (2014). *Team parenting for children in foster care,* London: Jessica Kingsley Publishers.

Chipungu, S. S. and Bent-Goodley, T. B. (2004). Meeting the challenges of contemporary foster care, *Future of Children,* 14(1), pp.75-93.

Chuang, E., Wells, R., Green, S. and Reiter, K. (2011). Performance-based contracting and the moderating influence of caseworker role overload on service provision in child welfare, *Administration in Social Work,* 35(5), pp.453-474.

Claiborne, N., Auerbach, C., Lawrence, C., Liu, J. McGowna, B.G. Fernendes, G. and Magnano, J. (2011). Child welfare agency climate influence on worker commitment, *Children and Youth Services Review,* 33(11), pp.2096-2102.

Clarke, H. (2009). *Getting the support they need: Findings of a survey of foster carers in the UK,* London: The Fostering Network.

Collis, A. (1999). Supporting foster carers, in A. Wheal, (Ed), *The RHP companion to foster care,* Lyme Regis: Russell House Publishing.

Cox, M. E., Buehler, C. and Orme, J. G. (2002). Recruitment and foster family service, *Journal of Sociology and Social Welfare,* 29(3), pp.151-177.

Department for Education (2011). *Fostering services: National Minimum Standards,* London: DfE.

Farmer, E., Moyers, S. and Lipscombe, J. (2004). *Fostering adolescents,* London: Jessica Kingsley Publishers.

Fisher, T., Gibbs, I., Sinclair, I. and Wilson, K. (2000). Sharing the care: The qualities sought of social workers by foster carers, *Child and Family Social Work,* 5(3), pp.225-233.

Fulcher, L. C. and McGladdery, S. (2011). Re-examining social work roles and tasks with foster care, *Child and Youth Services,* 32(1), pp.19-38.

Gleeson, J. P. and Philbin, C. M. (1996). Preparing case workers for practice in kinship foster care: The supervisor's dilemma, *The Clinical Supervisor,* 14(1), pp.19-34.

Green, J., Biehal, N., Roberts, C., Dixon, J., Kay, C., Parry, E., Rothwell, J., Roby, A., Kapadia, D., Scott, S. and Sinclair, I. (2014). Multidimensional treatment foster care for adolescents in English care: Randomised trial and observational cohort evaluation, *British Journal of Psychiatry,* 204, 1-8. doi: 10.1192/bjp.bp.113.131466 (Advance online publication).

H. M. Government (2011). *The Children Act 1989 guidance and regulations, Volume 4: Fostering services,* London: Department of Education.

Hawkins, P. and Shohet, R. (2012). *Supervision in the helping professions,* (4th edition), Milton Keynes: Open University Press.

Hollingsworth, L. D., Bybee, D., Johnson, E. I. and Swick, D. C. (2010). A comparison of caseworker characteristics in public and private foster care agencies, *Children and Youth Services Review,* 32(4), pp.578-584.

Hudson, P. and Levasseur, K. (2002). Supporting foster parents: Caring voices, *Child Welfare,* 81(6), pp.853 – 877.

Kirton, D., Beecham, J. and Ogilvie, K. (2007). Still the poor relations? Perspectives on valuing and listening to foster carers, *Adoption and Fostering,* 31(3), pp.6-17.

Lawson, D. (2011). *A foster care handbook for supervising social workers (England),* London: the Fostering Network.

Macgregor, T.E., Rodger, S. Cummings, A.L. and Leschied, A.W. (2006). The needs of foster parents: A qualitative study of motivation, support, and retention, *Qualitative Social Work* 5(3), pp.351-368.

Maclay, F., Bunce, M. and Purves, D. G. (2006). Surviving the system as a foster carer, *Adoption and Fostering,* 30(1), pp.29-38.

McSherry, D., Malet, M. F. and Weatherall, K. (2013). *Comparing long-term placements for young children in care: The care pathways and outcome study – Northern Ireland,* London: British Agencies for Adoption and Fostering.

Okeke, T. C., (2003). *Foster mothers' experiences and perceptions of their relationships with caseworkers,* Chicago: Unpublished PhD dissertation.

Pithouse, A., Young, C. and Butler, I. (2002). Training foster carers in challenging behaviour: A case study in disappointment, *Child and Family Social Work,* 7(3), pp.203-214.

Price, J. P., Chamberlain, P., Landsverk, J. and Reid, J. (2009). KEEP foster-parent training intervention: Model description and effectiveness, *Child and Family Social Work,* 14(2), pp.233-242.

Ramsay, D. (1996). Recruiting and retaining foster carers: Implications of a professional service in Fife, *Adoption and Fostering,* 20(1), pp.42-46.

Rhodes, K. W., Orme, J. G. and Buehler, C. (2001). A comparison of family foster parents who quit, consider quitting, and plan to continue fostering, *Social Service Review,* 75(1), pp.84-114.

Rosenwald, M. and Bronstein, L. (2008). Foster parents speak: Preferred characteristics of foster children and experiences in the role of foster parent, *Journal of Family Social Work,* 11(3), pp.287-302.

Rowe, J., Cain, H., Hundleby, M. and Keane, A. (1984). *Long-term foster care,* London: Batsford Academic and Educational/British Agencies for Adoption and Fostering.

Schofield, G. and Simmonds, J. (2013). Curriculum framework for continuing professional development (CPD) on Planning and supporting permanence: Reunification, family and friends care, long-term foster care, special guardianship and adoption, *The College of Social Work – CPD Guide on Planning and Supporting Permanence,* London: The College of Social Work.

Schofield, G. and Ward, E. with Warman, A., Simmonds, J. and Butler, J. (2008) *Permanence in foster carer,* London: British Agencies for Adoption and Fostering.

Sebba, J. (2012). *Why do people become foster carers?* Oxford: Rees Centre.

Sellick, C. (1999). The role of social workers in supporting and developing the work of foster carers, in M. Hill (Ed) *Signposts in fostering: Policy, practice and research issues,* London: British Agencies for Adoption and Fostering, pp.239-249.

Sellick, C. (2013). Foster-care commissioning in an age of austerity: The experiences and views of the independent provider sector in one English region, *British Journal of Social Work,* 1-17. doi: 10.10931/bjsw/bct046 (Advance online publication).

Sellick, C., Thoburn, J. and Philpot, T. (2004). *What works in adoption and foster care?* Barkingside: Barnardo's.

Sheldon, J. (2004). "We need to talk": A study of working relationships between field social workers and fostering link social workers in Northern Ireland, *Child Care in Practice,* 10(1), pp.20-38.

Sinclair, I. (2005). *Fostering now: Messages from research,* London: Jessica Kingsley Publishers.

Sinclair, I., Gibbs, I. and Wilson, K. (2004). *Foster carers: Why they stay and why they leave,* London: Jessica Kingsley Publications.

Sinclair, I., Wilson, K. and Gibbs, I. (2005). *Foster placements: Why they succeed and why they fail,* London: Jessica Kingsley Publications.

Taylor, B. J. and McQuillan, K. (2014). Perspectives of foster parents and social workers on foster placement disruption, *Child Care in Practice,* 20(2), pp. 232–249.

Tregeagle, S., Cox, E., Forbes, C., Humphreys, C. and O'Neill, C. (2011). Worker time and the cost of stability, *Children and Youth Services Review,* 33(7), pp.1149-1158.

Triseliotis, J., Borland, M. and Hill, M. (2000). *Delivering foster care,* London: British Agencies for Adoption and Fostering.

Triseliotis, J., Sellick, C. and Short, R. (1995), *Foster care: Theory and practice,* London: B. T. Batsford Ltd/British Agencies for Adoption and Fostering.

Wade, J., Sirriyeh, A. Kohli, R. and Simmonds, J. (2012). *Fostering unaccompanied asylum-seeking young people: Creating a family life across a 'world of difference',* London: British Association for Adoption and Fostering.

Wilson, K., Sinclair, I. and Gibbs, I. (2000). The trouble with foster care: The impact of stressful 'events' on foster carers, *British Journal of Social Work,* 30(2), pp.193-209.

Wilson, K., Sinclair, I., Taylor, C., Pithouse, A. and Sellick, C. (2004). *Fostering success: An exploration of the research literature in foster care. Knowledge review 5,* London: Social Care Institute for Excellence/Bristol: Policy Press.

Wires, E. M. (1954). Some factors in the worker-foster parent relationship, *Child Welfare,* 33, pp.8-9.

Wonnacott, J. (2012). *Mastering social work supervision,* London: Jessica Kingsley Publishers.

Appendix A

Table 1: Details of studies included in the review

Reference	Country	Number of participants	Methodology
Brown, Moraes and Mayhew (2005)	Canada	44 foster carers	Interview
Brown (2008)	Canada	63 foster carers	Interview
Brown, Rodgers and Anderson (2014)	Canada	68 foster family resource workers	Group Interview
Cavazzi, Guilfoyle and Sims (2010)	Australia	7 foster carers	Interview
Chuang, Wells, Green and Reiter (2011)	USA	92 foster carers, caseworkers, foster children	Interview
Clarke (2009)	UK	442 foster carers	On-line survey
Fisher, Gibbs, Sinclair and Wilson (2000)	UK	994 foster carers	Questionnaire
Gleeson and Philbin (1996)	USA	8 supervising social workers, 3 foster care programme directors	Interview
Hollingsworth, Bybee, Johnson and Swick (2010)	USA	82 caseworkers	Interview
Hudson and Levasseur (2002)	USA	66 foster carers, 10 caseworkers	Questionnaire and interview
Kirton, Beecham and Ogilvie (2007)	UK	1,181 foster carers (questionnaires), 21 fostering service managers (interviews), 139 foster carers (focus groups), 124 social workers (focus groups)	Questionnaire, focus group, interview
Macgregor, Rodger, Cummings and Leschied (2006)	Canada	54 foster carers	Focus group
Maclay, Bunce and Purves (2006)	UK	9 foster carers	Interview
Okeke (2003)	USA	30 foster carers	Focus group, interview, participant observation
Ramsay (1996)	UK	72 foster carers	Questionnaire
Rhodes, Orme and Buehler (2001)	USA	265 former foster carers, 252 current foster carers	Questionnaire, interview
Rosenwald and Bronstein (2008)	USA	13 foster carers	Focus group
Sheldon (2004)	UK	49 children's social workers (questionnaire), 10 supervising social workers (questionnaire), 9 children's social workers (interview), 4 supervising social workers (interview)	Questionnaire, interview
Sinclair, Gibbs and Wilson (2004)	UK	1528 foster carers (census), 994 foster carers (questionnaire)	Questionnaire, census
Taylor and McQuillan (2014)	UK	Service evaluation – 36 foster placement disruptions, involving foster carers, children's social worker and supervising social workers	Questionnaire
Tregeagle, Cox, Forbes, Humphreys and O'Neill (2011)	Australia	Social workers supporting 27 foster placements	Diary records
Triseliotis, Borland and Hill (2000)	UK	822 foster carers (questionnaires), 67 foster carers (interviews)	Questionnaire, interview